Welcome!

Discover the key to transforming your personal and professional life with this ultimate guide to achieving peak performance. This comprehensive workbook is designed to help you unlock the full potential of your productivity, goal setting, and execution skills, providing you with more details, facts, and higher semantic richness for better results in just 12 weeks. This workbook is a perfect companion to the book The 12 Week Year by Brian P Moran.

The concept of the 12 Week Year is based on the idea that traditional annual planning is often ineffective and that breaking your goals down into manageable 12-week increments can significantly improve your focus and accelerate your progress. As a result, the 12 Week Year creates a sense of urgency and aligns with the natural rhythm of our lives, allowing you to accomplish more in less time.

By working through this structured workbook, you will gain access to the following:
- Goal identification, effective planning, and consistency in execution.
- Practical exercises, activities, and interactive tools designed to help you develop the skills and habits necessary to become a great performer who consistently achieves results..
- Clarify your life vision and your ultimate goals.
- Space for reflection and self-assessment, allowing you to track your progress, learn from your experiences, and continually refine your strategies.

Don't let another year pass by without realizing your full potential for success. Embrace the power of the 12 Week Year and make a lasting, meaningful impact on your life and career.

We can't wait to guide you through the **Books Made Easy** process to help you apply the top rated professional books to your career and life!

Best,

The Books Made Easy Team

STEP ONE | SELF ASSESSMENT

If you could fully maximize your potential, what would be different for you?

_____

_____

_____

_____

When you look at your life, are there areas you feel you are falling short?

_____

_____

_____

_____

What are the things you know that if you did consistently would lead you to success?

_____

_____

_____

_____

What is preventing you from doing those things consistently?

_____

....

....

....

_____

Things to keep in mind as you continue with your 12-week plan:

- Execution is the single greatest differentiator for individuals that lead their industries.
- Not by working harder, but by focusing on the activities that matter most is the fastest track to success.
- Yearly goals can lead to procrastination. Everyday counts!

NOTES

_____

_____

_____

_____

_____

_____

_____

_____

_____

_____

STEP TWO | WHAT DO YOU WANT IN LIFE?

What do you want to achieve in life?

_____

_____

_____

_____

What legacy do you want to create?

_____

_____

_____

_____

What kind of fulfillment and income do you want from your career?

_____

_____

_____

_____

What do you want for yourself and your family?

_____

_____

_____

_____

What interest and hobbies do you want to pursue?

_____

_____

_____

_____

What do you want to be known for?

_____

_____

_____

_____

STEP THREE | ESTABLISHING YOUR VISION

To perform at top level you need a vision that is compelling.
You need a vision of the future that is bigger than the present and you must be emotionally connected to that vision.

Who do you want to be/have/do in all areas of your life?

1. Business:

2. Personal:

3. Physical:

4. Community:

5. Family:

6. Key relationships:

7. Spiritual:

Aspirational vision: Be bold- Create a life vision that inspires you.

_____

_____

_____

_____

What do you want to create over the next 3 years?

_____

_____

_____

_____

NOTES

STEP FOUR | DEVELOP THE PLAN

- Identify the actions that you will need to take to achieve your goals.
- Determine your tactics. The daily tasks that will drive attainment of your goals.
- Tactics must be specific, actionable and include dates.
- Your 12 week plan needs to be aligned with your long term vision.
- You can only control your actions, not your results.
- A good plan fosters solid execution.
- Look at every area of life as we need a balance in order to be our best.

List all of the things you want | Dreams | Hopes |Desires

Have	Do	Be

As you start to list your 12 week goals remember to:

1. Make them **specific and measurable**. The more specific you can be the better.

2. State them **positively**. Focus on what you want to happen that is positive. Instead of focusing on a 2% error rate, focus on a 98% accuracy rate.

3. Ensure they are a **realistic stretch**. If. you can already easily achieve your goals its too easy, but if its so far from where you are now, scale it back.

4. Assign **accountability**. If you are not a part of a team, accountability is all yours.

5. Be **time-bond.** Deadline creates urgency. Each goal should have an end date/week.

STEP FOUR | DEVELOP THE PLAN

12-Week Goals:

_____

_____

_____

_____

Goal 1: _____

Tactics: The activities and actions you need to complete	Due Date

Goal 2: _____

Tactics: The activities and actions you need to complete	Due Date

STEP FOUR | DEVELOP THE PLAN

Goal 3: _____

Tactics: The activities and actions you need to complete	Due Date

Goal 4: _____

Tactics: The activities and actions you need to complete	Due Date

Goal 5: _____

Tactics: The activities and actions you need to complete	Due Date

NOTES

STEP FIVE | WEEKLY PLAN

- Spend the first 15-20 minutes of each week reviewing the progress from the past week and plan the current week.
- The weekly plan is the instrument that organizes and focuses your week.
- Your plan captures the actions due each week that are needed to reach your 12 week goal.
- You will need Lead and Lag indicators.
- Lag indicators are the results you want.
- Lead indicators are the activities that produce the results.

Weekly routine process:
1. Score your week: This is your indicator of success.
2. Check off each item you completed that week.
3. A score of 85% or more means you are on track.
4. Remember to be patient- look for improvement not perfection.

For each goal mark the percentage of achievement. For example if you achieved 100% then you would check the box for 10.

Goals		1	2	3	4	5	6	7	8	9	10	
Goal #1	No real progress											Achieved goal
Goal #2	No real progress											Achieved goal
Goal #3	No real progress											Achieved goal
Goal #4	No real progress											Achieved goal
Goal #5	No real progress											Achieved goal

What areas are you pleased with?

_____

_____

STEP FIVE | WEEKLY PLAN

What do you need to improve?

_____

_____

_____

_____

What obstacles did you encounter?

_____

_____

_____

_____

How can you overcome the obstacles?

_____

_____

_____

_____

Celebrate each win. What are some things you can use as rewards after completing a goal and or successful week?

_____

_____

_____

NOTES

STEP SIX | TIME MANAGEMENT

- What keeps most people from being exceptional is not a lack of time, but the way they allocate time.
- Effective time use is the difference between mediocre and great performance.
- Studies show that after being distracted from a serious task, it takes an average of 15 minutes to get back to the original task.

How are you currently spending your time? Conduct a time audit for this week:

	Sunday	Monday	Tuesday	Wednesday	Thursday	Friday	Saturday
7:00 am							
8:00 am							
9:00 am							
10:00 am							
11:00 am							
12:00 pm							
1:00 pm							
2:00 pm							
3:00 pm							
4:00 pm							
5:00 pm							
6:00 pm							
7:00 pm							

What did you notice about your week?

- What are the things that distract you the most?
- What tasks do you tend to procrastinate on?
- Do you consistently do the things that are most important?
- When are you most productive?
- What are you best time management habits?
- What adjustments willl you need to make?

*** Full size schedule page in bonus material section - page 30

STEP SIX | TIME BLOCKING

- We will not try to eliminate low value activities.
- Instead we will focus on carving out time to focus on high value activities.
- Pencil your time blocks starting with your strategic blocks, followed by buffer blocks, then your breakout block. After that add everything else to your schedule.

Use the template below to map out the following 5 steps:
- Block 15 minutes Monday morning to review and plan week.
- Schedule your 3 hour strategic block.
- Schedule one or two buffer blocks.
- Schedule a breakout block.
- Schedule all additional important activities
  - Meetings.
  - Marketing.
  - Prospecting.
  - Administrative work.
  - Personal tasks.

	Sunday	Monday	Tuesday	Wednesday	Thursday	Friday	Saturday
7:00 am							
8:00 am							
9:00 am							
10:00 am							
11:00 am							
12:00 pm							
1:00 pm							
2:00 pm							
3:00 pm							
4:00 pm							
5:00 pm							
6:00 pm							
7:00 pm							

*** Full size schedule page in bonus material section - page 30

NOTES

STEP SEVEN | ACCOUNTABILITY

- Most people point fingers when they experience setbacks. Something or someone else caused their failure. Our culture supports the victim mentality.
- By pointing fingers you become a victim and allow your success to be limited by external circumstances, people, or events, forfeiting all power to the unknown.
- Accountability allows you to take control of your life, to shape your destiny and fulfill your potential.
- Accountability is simply taking ownership of your actions and your results.

Resolve never to be the victim again. Notice when you are making excuses. Focus on the things YOU can control.

_____

_____

_____

_____

Stop feeling sorry for yourself. Feeling sorry produces self-pity. Learn to manage your thinking and attitude to setbacks.

_____

_____

_____

_____

NOTES

STEP EIGHT | MANTAINING MOMENTUM

Staying motivated: Use this exercise to identify what motivates you and create a plan to stay motivated throughout the 12 weeks.

_____

_____

_____

_____

Sometimes rewarding yourself for small victories keeps you on track. Identify small milestones you can celebrate with a corresponding reward.

_____

_____

_____

_____

What are somethings that might tempt you or disrupt your 12 weeks? How can you make those things or actions more difficult to do or have?

_____

_____

_____

_____

NOTES

STEP NINE | IDENTIFYING SKILL GAPS

Growth is essential for success. What are your strengths, weaknesses and top skills?

_____

_____

_____

_____

When you envision your career and the person you want to be, what skills, knowledge, strengths and skills, must the you of the future have?

_____

_____

_____

_____

What skills are you missing? What can you do to develop those skills and expand your areas of opportunity?

_____

_____

_____

_____

NOTES

STEP TEN | PERSONAL COMMITMENTS

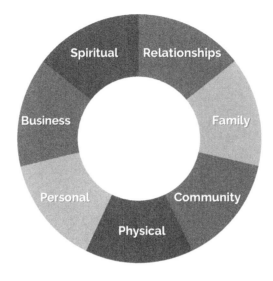

12 Week Goal Statements

_____

....

....

Key Stone Actions

_____

....

....

Commitment Cost

_____

....

....

STEP TEN | PERSONAL COMMITMENTS

☐   Are you emotionally bound to your commitments?

What are your Conscious intended intentions?

_____

....

....

What are your unconscious hidden intentions?

_____

....

....

Are there conflicts between your conscious stated intentions and your unconscious hidden intentions?

_____

....

....

Have you reconciled your conscious stated intentions and your unconscious hidden intentions?

_____

....

....

NOTES

STEP ELEVEN | REVIEWING YOUR PROGRESS

Schedule time for your weekly review. Put in on your calendar. Write here: when/how/what/when.

_____

....

....

Schedule a 6 week review. Evaluate and make adjustments. Put in on your calendar now and plan the details here: What/when/where/how.

_____

....

....

Remember you will go through the Valley of despair at some point. Stay strong and develop a plan to get through it.

_____

....

....

Schedule a 13 week review. Asses what when well and what needs adjustment. Also schedule time to recharge before starting your next 12 weeks. Write here any details that can help you stay focused.

....

....

....

Bonus Material

DAILY HABITS

MORNING ROUTINE

	M	T	W	T	F	S	S
....	◯	◯	◯	◯	◯	◯	◯
....	◯	◯	◯	◯	◯	◯	◯
....	◯	◯	◯	◯	◯	◯	◯
....	◯	◯	◯	◯	◯	◯	◯
....	◯	◯	◯	◯	◯	◯	◯

AFTERNOON ROUTINE

	M	T	W	T	F	S	S
....	◯	◯	◯	◯	◯	◯	◯
....	◯	◯	◯	◯	◯	◯	◯
....	◯	◯	◯	◯	◯	◯	◯
....	◯	◯	◯	◯	◯	◯	◯

NIGHT ROUTINE

	M	T	W	T	F	S	S
....	◯	◯	◯	◯	◯	◯	◯
....	◯	◯	◯	◯	◯	◯	◯
....	◯	◯	◯	◯	◯	◯	◯
....	◯	◯	◯	◯	◯	◯	◯
....	◯	◯	◯	◯	◯	◯	◯

	Sunday	Monday	Tuesday	Wednesday	Thursday	Friday	Saturday
7:00 am							
8:00 am							
9:00 am							
10:00 am							
11:00 am							
12:00 pm							
1:00 pm							
2:00 pm							
3:00 pm							
4:00 pm							
5:00 pm							
6:00 pm							
7:00 pm							

THE PLAN FOR TODAY

TODAY'S AFFIRMATION

_____

I'M THANKFUL FOR

1. _____
2. _____
3. _____
4. _____

TODAY'S GOALS

1. _____
2. _____
3. _____

TOP PRIORITIES

1. _____
2. _____
3. _____

TO LEARN

_____

_____

_____

_____

TO-DO LIST

○ _____
○ _____
○ _____
○ _____
○ _____
○ _____
○ _____
○ _____
○ _____
○ _____
○ _____
○ _____
○ _____
○ _____
○ _____
○ _____
○ _____
○ _____
○ _____
○ _____
○ _____
○ _____
○ _____
○ _____

WATER

☐ ☐ ☐ ☐ ☐ ☐ ☐ ☐
☐ ☐ ☐ ☐ ☐ ☐ ☐ ☐

TOMORROW'S GOALS

1. _____
2. _____
3. _____

GRATITUDE JOURNAL

MOOD

TODAY AFFIRMATION

TODAY I'M GRATEFUL FOR

- ....
- ....
- ....
- ....
- ....

HABITS

	YES	NO
....	☐	☐
....	☐	☐
....	☐	☐
....	☐	☐
....	☐	☐
....	☐	☐
....	☐	☐

THINGS THAT MADE ME SMILE

HOW I HELP TI

NOTES AND PHOTOS OF THE DAY

HABIT TRACKER

HABIT	CHECKLIST
	① ② ③ ④ ⑤ ⑥ ⑦ ⑧ ⑨ ⑩ ⑪ ⑫ ⑬ ⑭ ⑮ ⑯ ⑰ ⑱ ⑲ ⑳ ㉑ ㉒ ㉓ ㉔ ㉕ ㉖ ㉗ ㉘ ㉙ ㉚ ㉛
	① ② ③ ④ ⑤ ⑥ ⑦ ⑧ ⑨ ⑩ ⑪ ⑫ ⑬ ⑭ ⑮ ⑯ ⑰ ⑱ ⑲ ⑳ ㉑ ㉒ ㉓ ㉔ ㉕ ㉖ ㉗ ㉘ ㉙ ㉚ ㉛
	① ② ③ ④ ⑤ ⑥ ⑦ ⑧ ⑨ ⑩ ⑪ ⑫ ⑬ ⑭ ⑮ ⑯ ⑰ ⑱ ⑲ ⑳ ㉑ ㉒ ㉓ ㉔ ㉕ ㉖ ㉗ ㉘ ㉙ ㉚ ㉛
	① ② ③ ④ ⑤ ⑥ ⑦ ⑧ ⑨ ⑩ ⑪ ⑫ ⑬ ⑭ ⑮ ⑯ ⑰ ⑱ ⑲ ⑳ ㉑ ㉒ ㉓ ㉔ ㉕ ㉖ ㉗ ㉘ ㉙ ㉚ ㉛
	① ② ③ ④ ⑤ ⑥ ⑦ ⑧ ⑨ ⑩ ⑪ ⑫ ⑬ ⑭ ⑮ ⑯ ⑰ ⑱ ⑲ ⑳ ㉑ ㉒ ㉓ ㉔ ㉕ ㉖ ㉗ ㉘ ㉙ ㉚ ㉛
	① ② ③ ④ ⑤ ⑥ ⑦ ⑧ ⑨ ⑩ ⑪ ⑫ ⑬ ⑭ ⑮ ⑯ ⑰ ⑱ ⑲ ⑳ ㉑ ㉒ ㉓ ㉔ ㉕ ㉖ ㉗ ㉘ ㉙ ㉚ ㉛
	① ② ③ ④ ⑤ ⑥ ⑦ ⑧ ⑨ ⑩ ⑪ ⑫ ⑬ ⑭ ⑮ ⑯ ⑰ ⑱ ⑲ ⑳ ㉑ ㉒ ㉓ ㉔ ㉕ ㉖ ㉗ ㉘ ㉙ ㉚ ㉛
	① ② ③ ④ ⑤ ⑥ ⑦ ⑧ ⑨ ⑩ ⑪ ⑫ ⑬ ⑭ ⑮ ⑯ ⑰ ⑱ ⑲ ⑳ ㉑ ㉒ ㉓ ㉔ ㉕ ㉖ ㉗ ㉘ ㉙ ㉚ ㉛
	① ② ③ ④ ⑤ ⑥ ⑦ ⑧ ⑨ ⑩ ⑪ ⑫ ⑬ ⑭ ⑮ ⑯ ⑰ ⑱ ⑲ ⑳ ㉑ ㉒ ㉓ ㉔ ㉕ ㉖ ㉗ ㉘ ㉙ ㉚ ㉛
	① ② ③ ④ ⑤ ⑥ ⑦ ⑧ ⑨ ⑩ ⑪ ⑫ ⑬ ⑭ ⑮ ⑯ ⑰ ⑱ ⑲ ⑳ ㉑ ㉒ ㉓ ㉔ ㉕ ㉖ ㉗ ㉘ ㉙ ㉚ ㉛

NOTE

Our Final Message

Thank you for purchasing this workbook.

We hope you have the discipline and determination to achieve more in 12 weeks than most achieve in 12 months.

Remember to stay focused on your vision and celebrate your wins along the way. Good luck! You got this!

Look for progress not perfection.

This workbook is designed to be a companion to the book The 12 Week Year by Brian P Moran.

Printed in Great Britain
by Amazon